G000089585

SPIRIT OF

EXMOOR

PETER HENDRIE

First published in Great Britain in 2007, reprinted 2010

British Library Cataloguing-in-Publication Data
A CIP record for this title is available from the British Library

ISBN 978 0 85710 003 0

PiXZ Books
Halsgrove House, Ryelands Industrial Estate,
Bagley Road, Wellington, Somerset TA21 9PZ
Tel: 01823 653777
Fax: 01823 216796
email: sales@halsgrove.com

An imprint of Halstar Ltd, part of the Halsgrove group of companies
Information on all Halsgrove titles is available at: www.halsgrove.com

Printed and bound in China by Toppan Leefung Printing Ltd

Introduction

Exmoor is the second smallest of England's National Parks, barely 267 square miles. Nevertheless, it possesses some of the most diverse and spectacular landscapes to be found anywhere in the country. The steep-sided combes with fast-flowing streams, the glorious freedom of the coast, the vibrant colours of heather woodland punctuated by vivid yellow gorse, and the serenity of its southern wooded valleys, all conspire to produce a special magic that is uniquely Exmoor's.

The wildlife, too, adds a distinctive element to the Exmoor scenery. This is especially so of the native Exmoor pony – one of the rarest and most ancient breeds in the world – and the wild red deer, the proud and fitting symbol of the National Park.

Stag, Hinds and Calves
Wild red deer grazing on the slopes of Dunkery Beacon.

Opposite page:
Snow-covered Barrows
At 428 metres above sea level, Brightworthy Barrows
don their wintry coat with a soft pink hue.

A Splash of Colour
Seen here at Webber's Post, irresistible blooms of yellow
gorse add striking bolts of colour across the moorland.

Wintry Glow
A rosy-pink glow adds warmth to the snow-dusted landscape.
Blackford Combe near Nutscale, on a chilly winter's eve.

Meadow of Bluebells
A wash of blue cascades down a spring green meadow at
Harwood Plantation, close to Wheddon Cross.

Isolated Foxgloves
Four crimson foxgloves highlighted in a sea of green meadow grass and bulrushes.

Overleaf:
Watermouth, Hangman and Beyond
A panoramic view across Watermouth Cove, with the dramatic hogs-backed cliffs of Little Hangman and Great Hangman dominating the background.

Tumbling Down

A pretty stream trips its
way, twisting and tumbling,
from Easter Hill into
East Water valley at
Cloutsham. Truly one
of Exmoor's most
attractive locations.

Selworthy Village
One of many typical thatched cottages to be found
in the picturesque village of Selworthy.

Setting Sun
A golden globe,
framed perfectly
between the trees
of Hillhead Cross,
Exford.

Opposite page:
**Tearooms
at Horner**
Quaint country
cottages in the
picturesque hamlet
of Horner.

15

Moving On
A parade of stags makes its way along Langcombe Head
near Dunkery in the early evening.

Gulley
Sunset, over an Exmoor seascape, rough, rugged and dramatic.
Distinctive of the coastal fringes of north-west Exmoor.

Looking Out Over the Punchbowl

A storm passes by Withycombe Farm near Winsford.
The Punchbowl is in the foreground with a blended
patchwork of fields stretching out in the distance.

The Valley of Rocks
From the top of Castle Rock looking over Rugged Jack and the Warren bathed in the warm glow of an autumn sunset. The famous cricket ground in the distance and a car give a sense of scale.

Prayway Head
The last light from a winter's sunset illuminates the moorland about Prayway Head.
The River Exe meanders through the softly undulating combe.

Fisherman's Cottage at Porlock Weir
Enveloped by a traditional stone wall, and
accentuated by the upturned hull of a wooden boat,
the cottage has a dateless presence.

Overleaf:
Robber's Bridge
A panoramic view of Robber's Bridge over fast-flowing Weir Water, in autumn colours.

Tearooms at Watersmeet
Where Hoaroak Water and the East Lyn river meet,
flowing rapidly through dark glens, rushing to the sea at Lynmouth.

Opposite page:
Breakwater at Porlock Weir
The clouds seem to mimic the white wash of the water
in the foreground on this very dramatic day.

Winter River
The River Barle flows rapidly, swollen by overnight rain.

Ray of Hope
Late-afternoon light bathes the church at Simonsbath
in a warm welcoming glow, yet also highlights
the two gates which lead to the church door.

Overleaf:
The Valley of Rocks
Panoramic view of the Valley of Rocks shrouded in late-autumn light.

The Beech Trees Over Copper Hill Linhay – the Magnificent Seven
The high midday sun throws a shadow to form an interesting foreground detail.

Lyncombe Farmstead
Tucked in a small valley, this isolated farmstead
has changed little in character over the years.

Autumn Beech

The majestic presence and regal colours of the beech coppice woods which have become a feature of the Exmoor landscape.

Cover-up
Sea mist hugs
the coastline of
Bossington
Hill and Selworthy
Beacon, with
Hurlstone
Point showing
through.

Emerald Green

Often a landscape can
be found literally by
your feet. This one is
at Robber's Bridge,
where a lichen-clad twig
lies at the base of a
moss-covered
beech trunk.

Fire and Water
A ray of sunlight
sets ablaze the
beech leaves on an
overhanging branch
which rests above
the East Lyn river
at Brendon.

Sunset Over Scob Hill
Untroubled, cattle feed on Scob Hill, in the lingering light of evening.

Framed Castle
A solitary oak makes a perfect frame for Dunster Castle, seen from the Deer Park near Carhampton Gate.

Overleaf:
Watermouth Harbour
A panoramic view of Watermouth Harbour.

Dunster Castle
Dunster Castle in the distance shares the prominence
of place with a birch tree growing oddly askew.

Castle Rock

Dominating the coastline, Castle Rock's ashen silhouette contrasts with the pale blue cloud-filled sky shot with bolts of pink, becoming an austere landmark in the twilight.

Still Grazing
Scattered sheep grazing
in the pastures above
Sherracombe Woods,
near Yarde Down.

'Des Res'
One of the many desirable stone barns found
across Exmoor, fully air conditioned.

Landacre Bridge

One of Exmoor's most popular spots, this well-preserved medieval bridge spans the River Barle near Withypool Common.

Rolling In
The layering of light gives
depth to the vibrant mixture
of intense colours,
which is emphasised by
the white sea mist acting
as a background canvas.

Exmoor Foals in Springtime
The young Exmoor foals, grouped under a blackthorn tree
in its full bloom, set the perfect springtime picture.

Woody Bay

This dramatic coastline on the northern edge of Exmoor revels in the last light of day, with the Valley of Rocks on the distant horizon.

Overleaf:
Porlock Vale

One of the most spectacular vistas on Exmoor, Porlock Vale stretches around to Hurlstone Point.

Chetsford Water

Looking through the floodgate towards Hurdle Down and
Almsworthy Common, the start of Chetsford Water,
a soft cover of snow cocoons the land.

Opposite page:
Good Night

Radiating the last rays of light and warmth the sun slips beneath the horizon,
enhancing the dark jagged rocks and illuminating the sea.

Purple Dome
A rhododendron bush near Chagford Farm
hugs the banks of Badgworthy Water.

Doone Country
A pitted path wends
its way into the
mysterious
Doone Valley,
with Badgworthy
in the distance.

The Old Horse Bridge
The Old Horse Bridge
spans the River Barle
between Brewer's Castle
and Mounsey Castle.

Landacre Bridge

Looking upstream, into
the crimson after-glow
of the evening sunset.

Twilight over Lynton

A magical time viewed from the top of Wind Hill, just as the twinkle of lights becomes visible in the final radiance of day.

Tarr Steps
One of the oldest and certainly most mysterious bridges on Exmoor, if not Britain.

Overleaf:
View Over Sherdon Hutch
The crisp texture and symmetry of the hedge serve to highlight the gently undulating combes in the soft evening light.

Malmsmead
The gentle flow of
Badgworthy Water,
giving this scene a
tranquil feel, as it trips
across the ford.

Mares and Foals
Exmoor ponies with their foals graze unhindered, as dusk approaches on Winsford Hill.

Barle River

As the soft, milky water bubbles over rocks in the foreground, the eye is led back to the foot of Cow Castle, in the right middle distance.

Long Curve
Looking across to
Heale from
Trentishoe Down
as the sun descends
casting its last rays
of light across
distant fields.

Long and Windy Path

The exposed path labours around the contours of the coastline as they dip and climb North Cleave, High Cliff, East Cleave and around to Heddon's Mouth.